Walt Disney's
Farmer
Mickey

GROLIER
BOOK CLUB EDITION

Every morning Farmer Mickey goes into the barn and milks the cow.

"Pshht, pshht!" goes the milk as it hits the pail.

The cow spends the day eating grass
in the pasture.

Then Mickey milks her again at night.

Every morning Minnie feeds a mushy corn cereal to the mother pig.

The piglets are still too young to eat cereal.

They drink their mother's milk.

Mickey visits the henhouse every day.
First he throws some corn to the chickens.
Then he looks in the hens' nests for eggs.
He gathers most of the eggs to eat.
But he leaves some eggs to hatch into chicks.

Something always needs fixing on a farm.
Uh-oh! There's a hole in the henhouse!

Mickey nails a new board to the wall.
Now the chickens can not get out.

The sheep stay in their pasture
day and night.
Sometimes a little lamb gets out.
Then Mickey finds it and brings it
back to its mother.

In the springtime Mickey plows
his fields.

Plowing loosens the soil and buries
the weeds.

Now the fields can be planted.

In one field Mickey grows corn.

First he plants the seeds.

Rain helps the seeds to grow into plants.

Mickey chops out the weeds with a hoe.

The corn grows taller than Mickey!

When the ears of corn are ripe, Mickey picks them.

He and Minnie eat some of the corn.

But the farm animals eat most of it.

In one field Mickey lets the
grass grow very tall.
Then he cuts the grass and
lets it dry.
The dried grass is called hay.
Mickey and Minnie gather
the hay and take it to the barn.

In the winter they feed the hay to
the horse and cow and sheep.

Mickey and Minnie have
a big vegetable garden.

Here are some of the vegetables they grow:
cabbage and tomatoes
sweet red peppers
carrots and onions

The goat is always getting into the garden.
He will eat anything—even the scarecrow!
"Get out of there!" yells Minnie.

In the fall the apples ripen.
Mickey picks the apples.
Minnie makes apple pies.
Yum!

Minnie has a roadside stand.
Every afternoon she sells things that are made or grown on the farm.
What a lot of good things!